*This Journal is dedicated
to the memory of...*

---

*Missing you eternally,
and with Love always...*

Introduction

The loss of a loved one.

It's something that almost everyone must deal with at some point in their lives.

And though everyone deals with loss and the grief that accompanies it differently, there are several main components or stages that we all must go through for us to recover and eventually move forward from the trauma of losing someone that we love.

The emotions that come along with such a life-changing event are almost always intense and oftentimes difficult to make sense of.

One simple yet effective way to sort through these emotions is to write them down.

This journal was designed specifically for people like you.

People who've lost someone important to them. Someone, who they loved dearly and couldn't imagine living their lives without.

But who, through no choice of their own must now find meaning in a world that suddenly makes no sense.

They must pick up the pieces and learn how to move on and begin living again.

There is no straight line through grief, and so similarly this journal wasn't designed to be worked front page to last.

There will be days when you don't feel like writing at all, and that's ok.

On the days when your emotions compel you to write, my advice is to open the journal and skim through the pages until you find a prompt that speaks to you and how you're feeling in the moment, then write.

Write as little or as much as you want just as long as you're getting the emotions out and onto the page where you can examine them in the light of reason.

And be sure to do the worksheet, it's yet another tool to help figure out where you're emotionally and what you want in that moment.

This journal was initially designed for a loved one who struggled recently after suffering a devastating loss.

My hope for you is that it will help you in your time of grief as well.

...In loving memory of those that we have lost.

The 5 Stages of Grief*

Denial	1
Anger	2
Bargaining	3
Depression	4
Acceptance	5

(*Based on Kübler-Ross 1967)

1.-A survival mechanism designed to help you deal with initial crushing blow of the loss.

2.-Once the initial shock and numbness wears of you begin to live with the reality of your loss which bring about anger, why did this happen to me?

3.-In your desperation you begin to bargain, with life, with God, with reality.

4.-Once the reality sets in that the loss is permanent we sink to an emotional low withdrawing from life, feel numbing, and living in a fog of despair.

5.-You come to terms with your new reality and realize that though you've suffered a major loss you're going to be ok.

Grief Journaling Worksheet

Today is___________, and my grief recovery stage is___________

It's been___________________since we parted,

And today I...

Feel:____

____

____

Wish:____

____

____

Want:____

____

____

Will:____

____

____in
honor of your memory.
*(e.g.-try to smile more, try to cry less, hug someone who
needs it, climb that mountain we talked about climbing, have
a scoop of your favorite ice cream...etc)

With Love always,____

Today, what I am really missing the most is...

Grief Journaling Worksheet

Today is__________, and my grief recovery stage is___________

It's been___________________since we parted,

And today I...

Feel:____
____
____

Wish:____
____
____

Want:____
____
____

Will:____
____
____in
honor of your memory.
*(e.g.-try to smile more, try to cry less, hug someone who
needs it, climb that mountain we talked about climbing, have
a scoop of your favorite ice cream...etc)

With Love always,_____________________________________

The biggest lesson I have learned from the loss of
my loved one is...

Grief Journaling Worksheet

Today is__________, and my grief recovery stage is__________

It's been_____________________since we parted,

And today I...

Feel:____
____
____

Wish:____
____
____

Want:____
____
____

Will:____
____
____in
honor of your memory.
*(e.g.-try to smile more, try to cry less, hug someone who
needs it, climb that mountain we talked about climbing, have
a scoop of your favorite ice cream...etc)

With Love always,____

Something that I remember today about you is...

Grief Journaling Worksheet

Today is__________, and my grief recovery stage is___________

It's been__________________since we parted,

And today I...

Feel:____

____

____

Wish:____

____

____

Want:____

____

____

Will:____

____
____in
honor of your memory.
*(e.g.-try to smile more, try to cry less, hug someone who
needs it, climb that mountain we talked about climbing, have
a scoop of your favorite ice cream...etc)

With Love always,____

If I had a wish and could change one thing, it would be...

Grief Journaling Worksheet

Today is__________, and my grief recovery stage is___________

It's been___________________since we parted,

And today I...

Feel:____
____
____

Wish:____
____
____

Want:____
____
____

Will:____
____
____in
honor of your memory.
*(e.g.-try to smile more, try to cry less, hug someone who
needs it, climb that mountain we talked about climbing, have
a scoop of your favorite ice cream...etc)

With Love always,_____________________________________

How loving you has shaped/changed who I am...

Grief Journaling Worksheet

Today is__________, and my grief recovery stage is__________

It's been_________________since we parted,

And today I...

Feel:____
____
____

Wish:____
____
____

Want:____
____
____

Will:____
____
____in
honor of your memory.
*(e.g.-try to smile more, try to cry less, hug someone who
needs it, climb that mountain we talked about climbing, have
a scoop of your favorite ice cream...etc)

With Love always,____

In quiet times what I think most about is...

Grief Journaling Worksheet

Today is___________, and my grief recovery stage is___________

It's been___________________since we parted,

And today I...

Feel:____
____
____

Wish:____
____
____

Want:____
____
____

Will:____
____
____in
honor of your memory.
*(e.g.-try to smile more, try to cry less, hug someone who
needs it, climb that mountain we talked about climbing, have
a scoop of your favorite ice cream...etc)

With Love always,____

What really angers me about your being gone is...

Grief Journaling Worksheet

Today is__________, and my grief recovery stage is___________

It's been___________________since we parted,

And today I...

Feel:____

____

____

Wish:____

____

____

Want:____

____

____

Will:____

____

____in
honor of your memory.
*(e.g.-try to smile more, try to cry less, hug someone who
needs it, climb that mountain we talked about climbing, have
a scoop of your favorite ice cream...etc)

With Love always,_____________________________________

My very favorite thing we used to do was...

Grief Journaling Worksheet

Today is__________, and my grief recovery stage is___________

It's been___________________since we parted,

And today I...

Feel:____
____
____

Wish:____
____
____

Want:____
____
____

Will:____
____
____in
honor of your memory.
*(e.g.-try to smile more, try to cry less, hug someone who
needs it, climb that mountain we talked about climbing, have
a scoop of your favorite ice cream...etc)

With Love always,____

Now that you're are gone, I have resolved to…

Grief Journaling Worksheet

Today is__________, and my grief recovery stage is____________

It's been___________________since we parted,

And today I...

Feel:____
____
____

Wish:____
____
____

Want:____
____
____

Will:____
____
____in
honor of your memory.
*(e.g.-try to smile more, try to cry less, hug someone who
needs it, climb that mountain we talked about climbing, have
a scoop of your favorite ice cream...etc)

With Love always,____

How losing you has changed my life... In bed at night, my mind drifts to thoughts of...

Grief Journaling Worksheet

Today is__________, and my grief recovery stage is__________

It's been__________________since we parted,

And today I...

Feel:____
____
____

Wish:____
____
____

Want:____
____
____

Will:____
____
____in
honor of your memory.
*(e.g.-try to smile more, try to cry less, hug someone who
needs it, climb that mountain we talked about climbing, have
a scoop of your favorite ice cream...etc)

With Love always,____

The one thing I really wish I could ask you is...

Grief Journaling Worksheet

Today is__________, and my grief recovery stage is___________

It's been___________________since we parted,

And today I...

Feel:____
____
____

Wish:____
____
____

Want:____
____
____

Will:____
____
____in
honor of your memory.
*(e.g.-try to smile more, try to cry less, hug someone who
needs it, climb that mountain we talked about climbing, have
a scoop of your favorite ice cream...etc)

With Love always,_____________________________________

I remember your favorite song was always...

Grief Journaling Worksheet

Today is__________, and my grief recovery stage is___________

It's been___________________since we parted,

And today I...

Feel:____

____

____

Wish:____

____

____

Want:____

____

____

Will:____

____

____in
honor of your memory.
*(e.g.-try to smile more, try to cry less, hug someone who
needs it, climb that mountain we talked about climbing, have
a scoop of your favorite ice cream...etc)

With Love always,____________________________________

How things have changed since you've been gone...

Grief Journaling Worksheet

Today is__________, and my grief recovery stage is___________

It's been__________________since we parted,

And today I...

Feel:____
____
____

Wish:____
____
____

Want:____
____
____

Will:____
____
____in
honor of your memory.
*(e.g.-try to smile more, try to cry less, hug someone who
needs it, climb that mountain we talked about climbing, have
a scoop of your favorite ice cream...etc)

With Love always,____

My single most meaningful memory of you is...

Grief Journaling Worksheet

Today is__________, and my grief recovery stage is___________

It's been___________________since we parted,

And today I...

Feel:____
____
____

Wish:____
____
____

Want:____
____
____

Will:____
____
____in
honor of your memory.
*(e.g.-try to smile more, try to cry less, hug someone who
needs it, climb that mountain we talked about climbing, have
a scoop of your favorite ice cream...etc)

With Love always,____

My hope for me and everyone who loved you is...

Grief Journaling Worksheet

Today is___________, and my grief recovery stage is____________

It's been___________________since we parted,

And today I...

Feel:____
____
____

Wish:____
____
____

Want:____
____
____

Will:____
____
____in
honor of your memory.
*(e.g.-try to smile more, try to cry less, hug someone who
needs it, climb that mountain we talked about climbing, have
a scoop of your favorite ice cream...etc)

With Love always,______________________________________

My very first memory of you was...

Grief Journaling Worksheet

Today is____________, and my grief recovery stage is____________

It's been____________________since we parted,

And today I...

Feel:____
____
____

Wish:____
____
____

Want:____
____
____

Will:____
____
____in
honor of your memory.
*(e.g.-try to smile more, try to cry less, hug someone who
needs it, climb that mountain we talked about climbing, have
a scoop of your favorite ice cream...etc)

With Love always,____

First thing when I wake up in the morning…

Grief Journaling Worksheet

Today is__________, and my grief recovery stage is___________

It's been__________________since we parted,

And today I...

Feel:____
____
____

Wish:____
____
____

Want:____
____
____

Will:____
____
____in
honor of your memory.
*(e.g.-try to smile more, try to cry less, hug someone who
needs it, climb that mountain we talked about climbing, have
a scoop of your favorite ice cream...etc)

With Love always,__________________________________

Of everything, the thing I will miss the most is...

Grief Journaling Worksheet

Today is___________, and my grief recovery stage is____________

It's been_____________________since we parted,

And today I...

Feel:____

____

____

Wish:____

____

____

Want:____

____

____

Will:____

____

____in
honor of your memory.
*(e.g.-try to smile more, try to cry less, hug someone who
needs it, climb that mountain we talked about climbing, have
a scoop of your favorite ice cream...etc)

With Love always,____

Whenever I start to feel overwhelmed by my emotions, I'll remember this one thing about you that'll bring me comfort... The thing I will miss most of all is...

Grief Journaling Worksheet

Today is__________, and my grief recovery stage is____________

It's been___________________since we parted,

And today I...

Feel:____
____
____

Wish:____
____
____

Want:____
____
____

Will:____
____
____in
honor of your memory.
*(e.g.-try to smile more, try to cry less, hug someone who
needs it, climb that mountain we talked about climbing, have
a scoop of your favorite ice cream...etc)

With Love always,____

The most recent dream I had about you...

Grief Journaling Worksheet

Today is__________, and my grief recovery stage is__________

It's been__________________since we parted,

And today I...

Feel:____
____
____

Wish:____
____
____

Want:____
____
____

Will:____
____
____in
honor of your memory.
*(e.g.-try to smile more, try to cry less, hug someone who
needs it, climb that mountain we talked about climbing, have
a scoop of your favorite ice cream...etc)

With Love always,__________________________________

Whenever I was around you, I always felt...

Grief Journaling Worksheet

Today is__________, and my grief recovery stage is___________

It's been___________________since we parted,

And today I...

Feel:____
____
____

Wish:____
____
____

Want:____
____
____

Will:____
____
____in
honor of your memory.
*(e.g.-try to smile more, try to cry less, hug someone who
needs it, climb that mountain we talked about climbing, have
a scoop of your favorite ice cream...etc)

With Love always,______________________________________

The thing I'm having a hard time with in all of this is...

Grief Journaling Worksheet

Today is____________, and my grief recovery stage is____________

It's been__________________since we parted,

And today I...

Feel:____
____
____

Wish:____
____
____

Want:____
____
____

Will:____
____
____in
honor of your memory.
*(e.g.-try to smile more, try to cry less, hug someone who
needs it, climb that mountain we talked about climbing, have
a scoop of your favorite ice cream...etc)

With Love always,____

One thing you did that always made me laugh was...

Grief Journaling Worksheet

Today is__________, and my grief recovery stage is__________

It's been_______________since we parted,

And today I...

Feel:____
____
____

Wish:____
____
____

Want:____
____
____

Will:____
____
____in
honor of your memory.
*(e.g.-try to smile more, try to cry less, hug someone who
needs it, climb that mountain we talked about climbing, have
a scoop of your favorite ice cream...etc)

With Love always,____

Whenever this happens, I always think of you...

Grief Journaling Worksheet

Today is___________, and my grief recovery stage is____________

It's been___________________since we parted,

And today I...

Feel:____
____
____

Wish:____
____
____

Want:____
____
____

Will:____
____
____in
honor of your memory.
*(e.g.-try to smile more, try to cry less, hug someone who
needs it, climb that mountain we talked about climbing, have
a scoop of your favorite ice cream...etc)

With Love always,____

How I will continue coping with the loss of you
every day...

Grief Journaling Worksheet

Today is__________, and my grief recovery stage is__________

It's been__________________since we parted,

And today I...

Feel:____
____
____

Wish:____
____
____

Want:____
____
____

Will:____
____
____in
honor of your memory.
*(e.g.-try to smile more, try to cry less, hug someone who
needs it, climb that mountain we talked about climbing, have
a scoop of your favorite ice cream...etc)

With Love always,____

The greatest lesson you taught me was...

Grief Journaling Worksheet

Today is__________, and my grief recovery stage is___________

It's been___________________since we parted,

And today I...

Feel:____
____
____

Wish:____
____
____

Want:____
____
____

Will:____
____
____in
honor of your memory.
*(e.g.-try to smile more, try to cry less, hug someone who
needs it, climb that mountain we talked about climbing, have
a scoop of your favorite ice cream...etc)

With Love always,_____________________________________

For me, the hardest time of day is...

Grief Journaling Worksheet

Today is__________, and my grief recovery stage is___________

It's been___________________since we parted,

And today I...

Feel:____

____

____

Wish:____

____

____

Want:____

____

____

Will:____

____

____in
honor of your memory.
*(e.g.-try to smile more, try to cry less, hug someone who
needs it, climb that mountain we talked about climbing, have
a scoop of your favorite ice cream...etc)

With Love always,____

Whenever I was around you, no matter what you always made me feel...

Grief Journaling Worksheet

Today is__________, and my grief recovery stage is___________

It's been___________________since we parted,

And today I...

Feel:____

____

____

Wish:____

____

____

Want:____

____

____

Will:____

____

____in
honor of your memory.
*(e.g.-try to smile more, try to cry less, hug someone who
needs it, climb that mountain we talked about climbing, have
a scoop of your favorite ice cream...etc)

With Love always,____

If I could tell you one thing right now it would be...

____

____

____

____

____

____

____

____

____

____

____

____

Grief Journaling Worksheet

Today is_________, and my grief recovery stage is___________

It's been__________________since we parted,

And today I...

Feel:____
____
____

Wish:____
____
____

Want:____
____
____

Will:____
____
____in
honor of your memory.
*(e.g.-try to smile more, try to cry less, hug someone who
needs it, climb that mountain we talked about climbing, have
a scoop of your favorite ice cream...etc)

With Love always,_____________________________________

I know that eventually I will be okay because...

Grief Journaling Worksheet

Today is__________, and my grief recovery stage is___________

It's been__________________since we parted,

And today I...

Feel:____
____
____

Wish:____
____
____

Want:____
____
____

Will:____
____
____in
honor of your memory.
*(e.g.-try to smile more, try to cry less, hug someone who
needs it, climb that mountain we talked about climbing, have
a scoop of your favorite ice cream...etc)

With Love always,__________________________________

What is most helpful for me right now is...

Grief Journaling Worksheet

Today is__________, and my grief recovery stage is__________

It's been__________________since we parted,

And today I...

Feel:____
____
____

Wish:____
____
____

Want:____
____
____

Will:____
____
____in
honor of your memory.
*(e.g.-try to smile more, try to cry less, hug someone who
needs it, climb that mountain we talked about climbing, have
a scoop of your favorite ice cream...etc)

With Love always,____

To let these feelings progress naturally into something else, I will...

Grief Journaling Worksheet

Today is__________, and my grief recovery stage is___________

It's been__________________since we parted,

And today I...

Feel:____

____

____

Wish:____

____

____

Want:____

____

____

Will:____

____

____in
honor of your memory.
*(e.g.-try to smile more, try to cry less, hug someone who
needs it, climb that mountain we talked about climbing, have
a scoop of your favorite ice cream...etc)

With Love always,__________________________________

The little things you did that meant the most to
me were...

Grief Journaling Worksheet

Today is____________, and my grief recovery stage is____________

It's been____________________since we parted,

And today I...

Feel:____

____

____

Wish:____

____

____

Want:____

____

____

Will:____

____

____in
honor of your memory.
*(e.g.-try to smile more, try to cry less, hug someone who
needs it, climb that mountain we talked about climbing, have
a scoop of your favorite ice cream...etc)

With Love always,____________________________________

A tradition that I'll continue that helps me to remember...

Grief Journaling Worksheet

Today is__________, and my grief recovery stage is___________

It's been___________________since we parted,

And today I...

Feel:____
____
____

Wish:____
____
____

Want:____
____
____

Will:____
____
____in
honor of your memory.
*(e.g.-try to smile more, try to cry less, hug someone who
needs it, climb that mountain we talked about climbing, have
a scoop of your favorite ice cream...etc)

With Love always,_________________________________

I feel I can best honor you by...

Grief Journaling Worksheet

Today is__________, and my grief recovery stage is__________

It's been___________________since we parted,

And today I...

Feel:____
____
____

Wish:____
____
____

Want:____
____
____

Will:____
____
____in
honor of your memory.
*(e.g.-try to smile more, try to cry less, hug someone who
needs it, climb that mountain we talked about climbing, have
a scoop of your favorite ice cream...etc)

With Love always,____

The thing I could use some more of right now emotionally is...

Grief Journaling Worksheet

Today is__________, and my grief recovery stage is___________

It's been_____________________since we parted,

And today I...

Feel:____
____
____

Wish:____
____
____

Want:____
____
____

Will:____
____
____in
honor of your memory.
*(e.g.-try to smile more, try to cry less, hug someone who
needs it, climb that mountain we talked about climbing, have
a scoop of your favorite ice cream...etc)

With Love always,____

Our absolute favorite place was always...

Grief Journaling Worksheet

Today is__________, and my grief recovery stage is__________

It's been__________________since we parted,

And today I...

Feel:____
____
____

Wish:____
____
____

Want:____
____
____

Will:____
____
____in
honor of your memory.
*(e.g.-try to smile more, try to cry less, hug someone who
needs it, climb that mountain we talked about climbing, have
a scoop of your favorite ice cream...etc)

With Love always,____

It would be great if someone would just say...

Grief Journaling Worksheet

Today is___________, and my grief recovery stage is___________

It's been_____________________since we parted,

And today I...

Feel:____

____

____

Wish:____

____

____

Want:____

____

____

Will:____

____

____in
honor of your memory.
*(e.g.-try to smile more, try to cry less, hug someone who
needs it, climb that mountain we talked about climbing, have
a scoop of your favorite ice cream...etc)

With Love always,_________________________________

I can't help but cry whenever I remember…

Grief Journaling Worksheet

Today is__________, and my grief recovery stage is__________

It's been__________________since we parted,

And today I...

Feel:____

____

____

Wish:____

____

____

Want:____

____

____

Will:____

____
____in
honor of your memory.
*(e.g.-try to smile more, try to cry less, hug someone who
needs it, climb that mountain we talked about climbing, have
a scoop of your favorite ice cream...etc)

With Love always,______________________________

A little less…would be nice right now, because…

Grief Journaling Worksheet

Today is___________, and my grief recovery stage is___________

It's been___________________since we parted,

And today I...

Feel:____

____

____

Wish:____

____

____

Want:____

____

____

Will:____

____

____in
honor of your memory.
*(e.g.-try to smile more, try to cry less, hug someone who
needs it, climb that mountain we talked about climbing, have
a scoop of your favorite ice cream...etc)

With Love always,___________________________________

A color or colors that makes me think of you...

Grief Journaling Worksheet

Today is__________, and my grief recovery stage is__________

It's been__________________since we parted,

And today I...

Feel:____

____

____

Wish:____

____

____

Want:____

____

____

Will:____

____

____in
honor of your memory.
*(e.g.-try to smile more, try to cry less, hug someone who
needs it, climb that mountain we talked about climbing, have
a scoop of your favorite ice cream...etc)

With Love always,____

The way(s) that I feel like I'm healing every day...

Grief Journaling Worksheet

Today is___________, and my grief recovery stage is____________

It's been_____________________since we parted,

And today I...

Feel:____
____
____

Wish:____
____
____

Want:____
____
____

Will:____
____
____in
honor of your memory.
*(e.g.-try to smile more, try to cry less, hug someone who
needs it, climb that mountain we talked about climbing, have
a scoop of your favorite ice cream...etc)

With Love always,___________________________________

I can't help but smile whenever I remember…

Grief Journaling Worksheet

Today is__________, and my grief recovery stage is___________

It's been___________________since we parted,

And today I...

Feel:____

____

____

Wish:____

____

____

Want:____

____

____

Will:____

____

____in
honor of your memory.
*(e.g.-try to smile more, try to cry less, hug someone who
needs it, climb that mountain we talked about climbing, have
a scoop of your favorite ice cream...etc)

With Love always,___________________________________

Something small I could try today to make things
easier is...

Grief Journaling Worksheet

Today is___________, and my grief recovery stage is___________

It's been___________________since we parted,

And today I...

Feel:____

____

____

Wish:____

____

____

Want:____

____

____

Will:____

____

____in
honor of your memory.
*(e.g.-try to smile more, try to cry less, hug someone who
needs it, climb that mountain we talked about climbing, have
a scoop of your favorite ice cream...etc)

With Love always,____

No matter what this memory of you will always
make me smile...

Grief Journaling Worksheet

Today is__________, and my grief recovery stage is__________

It's been__________________since we parted,

And today I...

Feel:____
____
____

Wish:____
____
____

Want:____
____
____

Will:____
____
____in
honor of your memory.
*(e.g.-try to smile more, try to cry less, hug someone who
needs it, climb that mountain we talked about climbing, have
a scoop of your favorite ice cream...etc)

With Love always,__________________________________

If there was one thing I could change…

Grief Journaling Worksheet

Today is__________, and my grief recovery stage is___________

It's been__________________since we parted,

And today I...

Feel:____

____

____

Wish:____

____

____

Want:____

____

____

Will:____

____
____in
honor of your memory.
*(e.g.-try to smile more, try to cry less, hug someone who
needs it, climb that mountain we talked about climbing, have
a scoop of your favorite ice cream...etc)

With Love always,_________________________________

Something that would help this process would be
a little more...

Grief Journaling Worksheet

Today is___________, and my grief recovery stage is___________

It's been___________________since we parted,

And today I...

Feel:____
____
____

Wish:____
____
____

Want:____
____
____

Will:____
____
____in
honor of your memory.
*(e.g.-try to smile more, try to cry less, hug someone who
needs it, climb that mountain we talked about climbing, have
a scoop of your favorite ice cream...etc)

With Love always,_______________________________________

Who in my life could I ask for help, and what would I ask for specifically?

Grief Journaling Worksheet

Today is__________, and my grief recovery stage is___________

It's been___________________since we parted,

And today I...

Feel:____

____

____

Wish:____

____

____

Want:____

____

____

Will:____

____
____in
honor of your memory.
*(e.g.-try to smile more, try to cry less, hug someone who
needs it, climb that mountain we talked about climbing, have
a scoop of your favorite ice cream...etc)

With Love always,____

A memory that will probably always make me
cry...

Grief Journaling Worksheet

Today is___________, and my grief recovery stage is____________

It's been___________________since we parted,

And today I...

Feel:____

____

____

Wish:____

____

____

Want:____

____

____

Will:____

____

____in
honor of your memory.
*(e.g.-try to smile more, try to cry less, hug someone who
needs it, climb that mountain we talked about climbing, have
a scoop of your favorite ice cream...etc)

With Love always,___________________________________

My grief recovery support system is...

Grief Journaling Worksheet

Today is__________, and my grief recovery stage is___________

It's been___________________since we parted,

And today I...

Feel:____
____
____

Wish:____
____
____

Want:____
____
____

Will:____
____
____in
honor of your memory.
*(e.g.-try to smile more, try to cry less, hug someone who
needs it, climb that mountain we talked about climbing, have
a scoop of your favorite ice cream...etc)

With Love always,_____________________________________

A comforting memory that I hold onto of you is…

Grief Journaling Worksheet

Today is__________, and my grief recovery stage is___________

It's been___________________since we parted,

And today I...

Feel:____

____

____

Wish:____

____

____

Want:____

____

____

Will:____

____

____in
honor of your memory.
*(e.g.-try to smile more, try to cry less, hug someone who
needs it, climb that mountain we talked about climbing, have
a scoop of your favorite ice cream...etc)

With Love always,_______________________________________

I feel most connected to my loved one when
I...

Grief Journaling Worksheet

Today is__________, and my grief recovery stage is___________

It's been___________________since we parted,

And today I...

Feel:____

____

____

Wish:____

____

____

Want:____

____

____

Will:____

____
____in
honor of your memory.
*(e.g.-try to smile more, try to cry less, hug someone who
needs it, climb that mountain we talked about climbing, have
a scoop of your favorite ice cream...etc)

With Love always,______________________________________

Three things that you really loved...

Grief Journaling Worksheet

Today is_________, and my grief recovery stage is__________

It's been_______________since we parted,

And today I...

Feel:____

____

____

Wish:____

____

____

Want:____

____

____

Will:____

____

____in
honor of your memory.
*(e.g.-try to smile more, try to cry less, hug someone who
needs it, climb that mountain we talked about climbing, have
a scoop of your favorite ice cream...etc)

With Love always,____________________________________

I feel the greatest sadness when...

Grief Journaling Worksheet

Today is__________, and my grief recovery stage is___________

It's been__________________since we parted,

And today I...

Feel:____

____

____

Wish:____

____

____

Want:____

____

____

Will:____

____

____in
honor of your memory.
*(e.g.-try to smile more, try to cry less, hug someone who
needs it, climb that mountain we talked about climbing, have
a scoop of your favorite ice cream...etc)

With Love always,____

A comforting memory that I have of my loved
one is...

Grief Journaling Worksheet

Today is__________, and my grief recovery stage is__________

It's been__________________since we parted,

And today I...

Feel:____

____

____

Wish:____

____

____

Want:____

____

____

Will:____

____

____in
honor of your memory.
*(e.g.-try to smile more, try to cry less, hug someone who
needs it, climb that mountain we talked about climbing, have
a scoop of your favorite ice cream...etc)

With Love always,____

One thing you truly hated was…

Grief Journaling Worksheet

Today is___________, and my grief recovery stage is____________

It's been___________________since we parted,

And today I...

Feel:____

____

____

Wish:____

____

____

Want:____

____

____

Will:____

____

____in
honor of your memory.
*(e.g.-try to smile more, try to cry less, hug someone who
needs it, climb that mountain we talked about climbing, have
a scoop of your favorite ice cream...etc)

With Love always,_________________________________

Something I can do to reduce my sadness is...

Grief Journaling Worksheet

Today is__________, and my grief recovery stage is___________

It's been___________________since we parted,

And today I...

Feel:____

____

____

Wish:____

____

____

Want:____

____

____

Will:____

____

____in
honor of your memory.
*(e.g.-try to smile more, try to cry less, hug someone who
needs it, climb that mountain we talked about climbing, have
a scoop of your favorite ice cream...etc)

With Love always,______________________________

My loved one always had a way of making me
feel...

Grief Journaling Worksheet

Today is__________, and my grief recovery stage is___________

It's been_____________________since we parted,

And today I...

Feel:____

____

____

Wish:____

____

____

Want:____

____

____

Will:____

____

____in
honor of your memory.
*(e.g.-try to smile more, try to cry less, hug someone who
needs it, climb that mountain we talked about climbing, have
a scoop of your favorite ice cream...etc)

With Love always,_______________________________________

The smell of________________makes always me
think of you because...

Grief Journaling Worksheet

Today is__________, and my grief recovery stage is____________

It's been____________________since we parted,

And today I...

Feel:____

____

____

Wish:____

____

____

Want:____

____

____

Will:____

____
____in
honor of your memory.
*(e.g.-try to smile more, try to cry less, hug someone who
needs it, climb that mountain we talked about climbing, have
a scoop of your favorite ice cream...etc)

With Love always,____

One important lesson I have learned recently is...

Grief Journaling Worksheet

Today is___________, and my grief recovery stage is___________

It's been___________________since we parted,

And today I...

Feel:____
____
____

Wish:____
____
____

Want:____
____
____

Will:____
____
____in
honor of your memory.
*(e.g.-try to smile more, try to cry less, hug someone who
needs it, climb that mountain we talked about climbing, have
a scoop of your favorite ice cream...etc)

With Love always,_____________________________________

One way I can express what I'm feeling in a creative way would be to... When I listen to your favorite song it reminds me of...

Grief Journaling Worksheet

Today is__________, and my grief recovery stage is___________

It's been___________________since we parted,

And today I…

Feel:____

____

____

Wish:____

____

____

Want:____

____

____

Will:____

____

____in
honor of your memory.
*(e.g.-try to smile more, try to cry less, hug someone who
needs it, climb that mountain we talked about climbing, have
a scoop of your favorite ice cream…etc)

With Love always,____

A negative thought I would like to replace is...

Grief Journaling Worksheet

Today is___________, and my grief recovery stage is___________

It's been___________________since we parted,

And today I...

Feel:____
____
____

Wish:____
____
____

Want:____
____
____

Will:____
____
____in
honor of your memory.
*(e.g.-try to smile more, try to cry less, hug someone who
needs it, climb that mountain we talked about climbing, have
a scoop of your favorite ice cream...etc)

With Love always,____

The one way that I am most like my loved one
is...

Grief Journaling Worksheet

Today is__________, and my grief recovery stage is____________

It's been______________________since we parted,

And today I...

Feel:____

____

____

Wish:____

____

____

Want:____

____

____

Will:____

____

____in
honor of your memory.
*(e.g.-try to smile more, try to cry less, hug someone who
needs it, climb that mountain we talked about climbing, have
a scoop of your favorite ice cream...etc)

With Love always,____

The memories of you that stand out for me the
most...

Grief Journaling Worksheet

Today is____________, and my grief recovery stage is____________

It's been_________________since we parted,

And today I...

Feel:____

____

____

Wish:____

____

____

Want:____

____

____

Will:____

____

____in
honor of your memory.
*(e.g.-try to smile more, try to cry less, hug someone who
needs it, climb that mountain we talked about climbing, have
a scoop of your favorite ice cream...etc)

With Love always,_________________________________

A positive thought I would like to have more often is...

Grief Journaling Worksheet

Today is__________, and my grief recovery stage is__________

It's been__________________since we parted,

And today I...

Feel:____

____

____

Wish:____

____

____

Want:____

____

____

Will:____

____

____in
honor of your memory.
*(e.g.-try to smile more, try to cry less, hug someone who
needs it, climb that mountain we talked about climbing, have
a scoop of your favorite ice cream...etc)

With Love always,____

The best way that I can honor my loved one by...

Grief Journaling Worksheet

Today is__________, and my grief recovery stage is___________

It's been__________________since we parted,

And today I...

Feel:____

____

____

Wish:____

____

____

Want:____

____

____

Will:____

____

____in
honor of your memory.
*(e.g.-try to smile more, try to cry less, hug someone who
needs it, climb that mountain we talked about climbing, have
a scoop of your favorite ice cream...etc)

With Love always,_____________________________________

If I could go back in time, I would...

Grief Journaling Worksheet

Today is____________, and my grief recovery stage is____________

It's been____________________since we parted,

And today I...

Feel:____
____
____

Wish:____
____
____

Want:____
____
____

Will:____
____
____in
honor of your memory.
*(e.g.-try to smile more, try to cry less, hug someone who
needs it, climb that mountain we talked about climbing, have
a scoop of your favorite ice cream...etc)

With Love always,____

Whenever I start to feel overwhelmed by the emotion of losing my loved one I will remember this phrase, bible verse, or mantra to give me comfort...

Grief Journaling Worksheet

Today is__________, and my grief recovery stage is__________

It's been__________________since we parted,

And today I...

Feel:____
____
____

Wish:____
____
____

Want:____
____
____

Will:____
____
____in
honor of your memory.
*(e.g.-try to smile more, try to cry less, hug someone who
needs it, climb that mountain we talked about climbing, have
a scoop of your favorite ice cream...etc)

With Love always,__________________________________

Three words that describe you perfectly...and why...

Grief Journaling Worksheet

Today is___________, and my grief recovery stage is___________

It's been___________________since we parted,

And today I...

Feel:____

____

____

Wish:____

____

____

Want:____

____

____

Will:____

____

____in
honor of your memory.
*(e.g.-try to smile more, try to cry less, hug someone who
needs it, climb that mountain we talked about climbing, have
a scoop of your favorite ice cream...etc)

With Love always,____

For me the hardest part about losing you is...

Grief Journaling Worksheet

Today is___________, and my grief recovery stage is___________

It's been__________________since we parted,

And today I...

Feel:____

____

____

Wish:____

____

____

Want:____

____

____

Will:____

____

____in
honor of your memory.
*(e.g.-try to smile more, try to cry less, hug someone who
needs it, climb that mountain we talked about climbing, have
a scoop of your favorite ice cream...etc)

With Love always,_______________________________________

To me your best quality was always...

Grief Journaling Worksheet

Today is__________, and my grief recovery stage is__________

It's been__________________since we parted,

And today I...

Feel:____

____

____

Wish:____

____

____

Want:____

____

____

Will:____

____

____in
honor of your memory.
*(e.g.-try to smile more, try to cry less, hug someone who
needs it, climb that mountain we talked about climbing, have
a scoop of your favorite ice cream...etc)

With Love always,________________________________

Some of my most powerful grief triggers are…

Grief Journaling Worksheet

Today is__________, and my grief recovery stage is___________

It's been___________________since we parted,

And today I...

Feel:____

____

____

Wish:____

____

____

Want:____

____

____

Will:____

____

____in
honor of your memory.
*(e.g.-try to smile more, try to cry less, hug someone who
needs it, climb that mountain we talked about climbing, have
a scoop of your favorite ice cream...etc)

With Love always,____

How having you in my life changed my life...

Grief Journaling Worksheet

Today is__________, and my grief recovery stage is__________

It's been__________________since we parted,

And today I...

Feel:____

____

____

Wish:____

____

____

Want:____

____

____

Will:____

____

____in
honor of your memory.
*(e.g.-try to smile more, try to cry less, hug someone who
needs it, climb that mountain we talked about climbing, have
a scoop of your favorite ice cream...etc)

With Love always,_________________________________

What has changed most without you in my life
is...

Grief Journaling Worksheet

Today is___________, and my grief recovery stage is___________

It's been___________________since we parted,

And today I...

Feel:____

____

____

Wish:____

____

____

Want:____

____

____

Will:____

____

____in
honor of your memory.
*(e.g.-try to smile more, try to cry less, hug someone who
needs it, climb that mountain we talked about climbing, have
a scoop of your favorite ice cream...etc)

With Love always,____

Something I am still working on learning to accept is...

Grief Journaling Worksheet

Today is__________, and my grief recovery stage is___________

It's been_____________________since we parted,

And today I...

Feel:____

____

____

Wish:____

____

____

Want:____

____

____

Will:____

____

____in
honor of your memory.
*(e.g.-try to smile more, try to cry less, hug someone who
needs it, climb that mountain we talked about climbing, have
a scoop of your favorite ice cream...etc)

With Love always,____

Is there is someone else who is hurting during my grief process? If so, is there something I can do to bring them comfort?

Grief Journaling Worksheet

Today is__________, and my grief recovery stage is___________

It's been___________________since we parted,

And today I...

Feel:____
____
____

Wish:____
____
____

Want:____
____
____

Will:____
____
____in
honor of your memory.
*(e.g.-try to smile more, try to cry less, hug someone who
needs it, climb that mountain we talked about climbing, have
a scoop of your favorite ice cream...etc)

With Love always,____

One thing I learned about myself because of you...

Grief Journaling Worksheet

Today is___________, and my grief recovery stage is___________

It's been___________________since we parted,

And today I...

Feel:____

____

____

Wish:____

____

____

Want:____

____

____

Will:____

____

____in
honor of your memory.
*(e.g.-try to smile more, try to cry less, hug someone who
needs it, climb that mountain we talked about climbing, have
a scoop of your favorite ice cream...etc)

With Love always,___________________________________

Now that you are gone, I have vowed that I am going to...

____

____

____

____

____

____

____

____

____

____

____

____

____

Grief Journaling Worksheet

Today is____________, and my grief recovery stage is____________

It's been____________________since we parted,

And today I...

Feel:____

____

____

Wish:____

____

____

Want:____

____

____

Will:____

____

____in
honor of your memory.
*(e.g.-try to smile more, try to cry less, hug someone who
needs it, climb that mountain we talked about climbing, have
a scoop of your favorite ice cream...etc)

With Love always,____

If I could get the chance to say one thing to you,
it would be…

Grief Journaling Worksheet

Today is___________, and my grief recovery stage is____________

It's been_____________________since we parted,

And today I...

Feel:____

____

____

Wish:____

____

____

Want:____

____

____

Will:____

____

____in
honor of your memory.
*(e.g.-try to smile more, try to cry less, hug someone who
needs it, climb that mountain we talked about climbing, have
a scoop of your favorite ice cream...etc)

With Love always,____

My best grief/loss coping mechanism is...

Grief Journaling Worksheet

Today is___________, and my grief recovery stage is____________

It's been___________________since we parted,

And today I...

Feel:____

____

____

Wish:____

____

____

Want:____

____

____

Will:____

____

____in

honor of your memory.

*(e.g.-try to smile more, try to cry less, hug someone who needs it, climb that mountain we talked about climbing, have a scoop of your favorite ice cream...etc)

With Love always,______________________________________

A quote that sums you up perfectly is...

Grief Journaling Worksheet

Today is__________, and my grief recovery stage is___________

It's been___________________since we parted,

And today I...

Feel:____

____

____

Wish:____

____

____

Want:____

____

____

Will:____

____

____in
honor of your memory.
*(e.g.-try to smile more, try to cry less, hug someone who
needs it, climb that mountain we talked about climbing, have
a scoop of your favorite ice cream...etc)

With Love always,_______________________________________

The most painful feeling in all of this is...

Grief Journaling Worksheet

Today is___________, and my grief recovery stage is____________

It's been__________________since we parted,

And today I...

Feel:____

____

____

Wish:____

____

____

Want:____

____

____

Will:____

____in
honor of your memory.
*(e.g.-try to smile more, try to cry less, hug someone who
needs it, climb that mountain we talked about climbing, have
a scoop of your favorite ice cream...etc)

With Love always,________________________________

A way that I can express my feelings in a creative
way is by...

____

____

____

____

____

____

____

____

____

____

____

____

____

Grief Journaling Worksheet

Today is__________, and my grief recovery stage is__________

It's been__________________since we parted,

And today I...

Feel:____
____
____

Wish:____
____
____

Want:____
____
____

Will:____
____
____in
honor of your memory.
*(e.g.-try to smile more, try to cry less, hug someone who
needs it, climb that mountain we talked about climbing, have
a scoop of your favorite ice cream...etc)

With Love always,__________________________

In your absence, my biggest personal motivation is...

Grief Journaling Worksheet

Today is___________, and my grief recovery stage is____________

It's been_____________________since we parted,

And today I...

Feel:____

____

____

Wish:____

____

____

Want:____

____

____

Will:____

____

____in
honor of your memory.
*(e.g.-try to smile more, try to cry less, hug someone who
needs it, climb that mountain we talked about climbing, have
a scoop of your favorite ice cream...etc)

With Love always,____

In the next 30 days the one thing I want to accomplish is...

Grief Journaling Worksheet

Today is__________, and my grief recovery stage is__________

It's been__________________since we parted,

And today I...

Feel:____

____

____

Wish:____

____

____

Want:____

____

____

Will:____

____

____in
honor of your memory.
*(e.g.-try to smile more, try to cry less, hug someone who
needs it, climb that mountain we talked about climbing, have
a scoop of your favorite ice cream...etc)

With Love always,____

To help myself heal, I am willing to…

Grief Journaling Worksheet

Today is__________, and my grief recovery stage is___________

It's been___________________since we parted,

And today I...

Feel:____
____
____

Wish:____
____
____

Want:____
____
____

Will:____
____
____in
honor of your memory.
*(e.g.-try to smile more, try to cry less, hug someone who
needs it, climb that mountain we talked about climbing, have
a scoop of your favorite ice cream...etc)

With Love always,________________________________

One sentence that best describes you…

Grief Journaling Worksheet

Today is__________, and my grief recovery stage is___________

It's been____________________since we parted,

And today I...

Feel:____

____

____

Wish:____

____

____

Want:____

____

____

Will:____

____

____in
honor of your memory.
*(e.g.-try to smile more, try to cry less, hug someone who
needs it, climb that mountain we talked about climbing, have
a scoop of your favorite ice cream...etc)

With Love always,________________________________

When things get hard I know I can depend on...

Grief Journaling Worksheet

Today is__________, and my grief recovery stage is___________

It's been___________________since we parted,

And today I...

Feel:____

____

____

Wish:____

____

____

Want:____

____

____

Will:____

____

____in
honor of your memory.
*(e.g.-try to smile more, try to cry less, hug someone who
needs it, climb that mountain we talked about climbing, have
a scoop of your favorite ice cream...etc)

With Love always,___________________________________

I am still having a difficult time understanding...

Grief Journaling Worksheet

Today is__________, and my grief recovery stage is___________

It's been__________________since we parted,

And today I...

Feel:____

____

____

Wish:____

____

____

Want:____

____

____

Will:____

____

____in
honor of your memory.
*(e.g.-try to smile more, try to cry less, hug someone who
needs it, climb that mountain we talked about climbing, have
a scoop of your favorite ice cream...etc)

With Love always,____

One way that I can choose to love myself more is
by...

Grief Journaling Worksheet

Today is__________, and my grief recovery stage is___________

It's been__________________since we parted,

And today I...

Feel:____

____

____

Wish:____

____

____

Want:____

____

____

Will:____

____

____in
honor of your memory.
*(e.g.-try to smile more, try to cry less, hug someone who
needs it, climb that mountain we talked about climbing, have
a scoop of your favorite ice cream...etc)

With Love always,____

A negative thought or emotion that I am ready to
let go of...

Grief Journaling Worksheet

Today is__________, and my grief recovery stage is__________

It's been__________________since we parted,

And today I...

Feel:____

____

____

Wish:____

____

____

Want:____

____

____

Will:____

____
____in
honor of your memory.
*(e.g.-try to smile more, try to cry less, hug someone who needs it, climb that mountain we talked about climbing, have a scoop of your favorite ice cream...etc)

With Love always,______________________________

A negative thought or emotion that I am ready to let go of...